Sneakers

THE SHOES WE CHOOSE!

by Robert Young

99232

dP DILLON PRESS, INC.
Minneapolis, Minnesota 55415

For Tyler,
the best sneaker I know

Acknowledgments

Many thanks to the following for their information, support, and encouragement: Barry Bates, Bill Bowerman, Lynn Bruce, Stephanie Burchfield, Kim Cooper, Jim Cormier, Lisa Deneffe, Sebastian DiCasoli, Sue and Alan Dickman, the Donnelly family, Ron Duquette, Nelson Farris, Helene Fletcher, Brian Forik, Karen and Joe Forward, Todd Gilmer, Mike Hanner, Karen and Vic Hansen, Dean Harvey, Mike Friton, Ann Herrick, Donna Hill, Jeff Hollister, Alisa Koessler, Elise Klysa, Joe Lee, Jack Loe, Mike May, Tom McGuirk, Gary Meininger, Ann Marie Mills, Jennifer Murray, Rick Myhre, Elizabeth and Terry Oas, Craig Ota, Tom Philips, Ellen and Tom Powers, Heather Mara Rem, Art Rogers, Evan Rutter, Joyce Shea, Wilson Smith, Bob Szumowski, Judy VanGilson, Liza Voges, Anne York, Lewis Young, and Peggy Young. Special thanks also to: Tim Ford for a great idea; Shelley Sateren, my editor; and to Sara Young for believing in dreams.

Illustrations have been reproduced through the courtesy of: Adidas, Asics Tiger, Avia, Combe, Converse, L.A. Gear, the National Archives, New Balance, Nike, Dan Orr, Reebok, and Sears. Cover photo by Dayton's Advertising Photography.

Library of Congress Cataloging-in-Publication Data

Young, Robert, 1951-
    Sneakers : the shoes we choose / Robert Young.
        p.   cm.
    Includes index.
    Summary: Discusses the history, design, manufacturing, and popularity of sneakers.
    ISBN 0-87518-460-X
     1. Sneakers—Juvenile literature. [1. Sneakers. 2. Shoes.]
    I. Title.
    TS1017.Y68 1991
    685'.31—dc20   90-26473
                                               CIP
                                             AC

Dillon Press, Inc., 242 Portland Avenue South
Minneapolis, Minnesota 55415

Printed in the United States of America
1 2 3 4 5 6 7 8 9 10 00 99 98 97 96 95 94 93 92 91

Contents

1

Crazy About Sneakers

Take a look at your feet. Most likely, you're wearing sneakers. Sneakers? Well, you might not call them that. Maybe you call them by their brand names, such as Nikes, Reeboks, or L.A. Gears. Other people might call them tennis shoes, running shoes, or simply "shoes." If you live in England, you say "trainers," and if you live in Australia, you say "sand shoes." There are many names for this comfortable, lightweight footwear, but the general name—the one that has been used since 1873—is sneakers.

Fewer than fifty years ago, sneakers were simple shoes. Their soles were made of rubber, and their *uppers* were made of *canvas*, a heavy cloth woven from cotton. Today's sneakers, however, are far from simple. They are made of the latest materials, and they come in every color and style you can imagine.

Throughout the world, there are many names for this popular footwear.

There are many different types of sneakers today, and people of all ages are crazy about them. Kids wear them, and so do teenagers, adults, and senior citizens. There are even sneakers made for newborn babies!

Nine out of every ten Americans own at least one

People of all ages wear sneakers, even babies and toddlers.

pair of sneakers, and one out of ten wears them every single day. People play, work, and exercise in them. They even wear them when they want to dress up. Americans buy more than 150 million pairs of sneakers each year, which adds up to billions of dollars.

About one-third of all these sneakers wear out in less than a year. But they aren't thrown out as fast as they wear out. Most people keep their old sneakers for at least three months after buying a new pair. Some people keep them because they're still comfortable, or so they have an extra pair to wear. Others keep them

Millions of people wear sneakers for work and play. This girl wouldn't wear anything else when riding her bike!

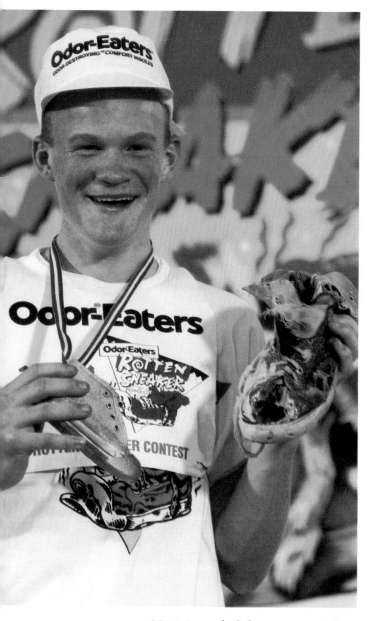

Matt Greenhalgh, winner of the 1990 Odor-Eaters International Rotten Sneaker Contest, holding his winning sneaker.

because throwing out old sneakers is like parting with old friends.

Many kids save their old sneakers and enter them in contests. The most famous contest for worn sneakers is the Odor-Eaters International Rotten Sneaker Contest. It's open to anyone under the age of 18 and is held each year in Montpelier, Vermont, on the first day of spring. Spring might be a time of new life and fresh air, but this contest is not. It's a time when kids from around the world show off their worn-out, stinky sneakers and hope to win prizes.

Judges carefully inspect the competing

sneakers for rips, tears, worn heels, and broken laces.

Smell, of course, counts, too. The owner of the worst pair of sneakers wins a $500 savings bond, a new pair of sneakers for every month of the year, and a year's supply of Odor-Eaters to keep his or her sneakers smelling fresh.

After the contest, the winning sneakers are set in a clear, airtight case and taken around the United States. The old shoes are put on display in shopping malls for thousands of people to see. At the end of a year's travel, the sneakers are placed in the Hall of Fumes, a rotten sneaker collection in Montpelier.

Not all sneaker collections are rotten. Some people, such as Ron Duquette in Oregon, collect sneakers from professional athletes. Ron started his collection nearly 15 years ago, when he was a ballboy for the Portland Trailblazers. Today, Ron has enough sneakers to fill a room. He has more than 170 signed pairs from players such as Isiah Thomas, Magic Johnson, and Jimmy Connors.

The Adidas Sports Shoe Museum in West Germany has an even larger collection of sneakers. It has more than 300 pairs, and other kinds of sports shoes, too. Much of this footwear was worn in important games or while breaking world records. Included in the collection are spikes that once belonged to track stars Jesse Owens, Billy Mills, Bob Hayes, and Edwin Moses.

Around the world, sneakers are everywhere you look—on feet, in contests, and even in museums. But that's not all. People wear sneaker jewelry and admire sneaker art, too. They also enjoy sneaker poems, songs, furniture, and birthday cakes. You can even talk to your friends on a sneaker telephone!

So how did this happen? How did sneakers come to be such an important part of our lives? It all started hundreds of years ago in the jungles of Central and South America, and the rest is history.

Ron Duquette with his signed sneakers collection.

Footnotes

■ The most popular color for sneakers is white.

■ Kids buy an average of 2 pairs of sneakers a year. Women buy an average of 1.5 pairs, and men buy an average of 1.3 pairs.

■ People who live in the states of Illinois, Indiana, Michigan, Ohio, and Wisconsin buy the most sneakers of all the people in the United States.

■ Matt Greenhalgh, 14, of Greenwich, Rhode Island, won the 1990 Odor-Eaters International Rotten Sneaker Contest.

■ Of all kids, 6 to 10 year olds own the most pairs of sneakers.

■ Americans spend about $2 billion each year on sneakers for kids. That is about twice as much as they spend on books for kids.

2 Sneakers' Early Days

For thousands of years, people have worn something on their feet. Cave dwellers strapped leaves, bark, and animal hides on their feet for protection. In later years, the Chinese wore shoes made of cloth, wood, and animal furs, and Greek and Roman soldiers wore leather sandals. There were many types of shoes in early times, but sneakers were not one of them.

In the 1600s, the Indian peoples of Central and South America helped to develop sneakers. They discovered a white sap oozing from the cahuchu (ka-OO-choo) tree. The people used this sap to make bouncing balls and waterproof bottles. They also dipped their feet in large bowls of it. When it dried, they had thin pairs of waterproof and insect-proof shoes.

When Christopher Columbus came to the Ameri-

Central and South Americans dipped their feet in cahuchu tree sap to make waterproof shoes.

cas, he took samples of this interesting sap back to Europe. For the next 200 years, many scientists tried to find ways to use it. Finally, in 1770, an English chemist named Joseph Priestly discovered that the sap could be used as an eraser to rub off pencil marks. After that, people started calling it "rubber."

There were many uses for rubber besides erasing, but there were problems with it, too. In cold weather, the rubber became hard and brittle. When the weather was hot, it became sticky and soft.

Many people tried to solve these problems. One man who tried was Charles Goodyear, an inventor from Connecticut. Goodyear tried adding chemicals to the rubber so that it might be more useful in all weather conditions and last longer, too.

One February night in 1839, Goodyear was experimenting in his kitchen. He added *sulphur*, a yellow mineral, to some rubber. Then, by accident, he dropped the mixture onto the top of his hot stove. Goodyear was too busy at the moment to clean it up. When he cleaned the mess later, he was surprised. The mixture was smooth and dry and could bend very easily.

But what would happen when the rubber became cold? Goodyear decided to find out. He nailed the piece of rubber outside his door on that freezing February night. In the morning, he could still bend the mixture easily!

Charles Goodyear had discovered a way to make rubber more useful in all weather conditions, by mixing it with sulphur and then heating it. This process is called *curing* or *vulcanizing*.

By the mid-1800s, shoemakers began to use rubber in their craft. At first, they just glued bands of it onto shoes for decoration. But soon, soles were made of rubber, too. These soles were lightweight, comfortable, and easy to walk in.

In the 1860s, for the first time, croquet shoes were made with rubber soles to help prevent damage to croquet courts. These shoes had

Charles Goodyear, inventor.

BLACK TENNIS OXFORDS.

No. 31470. Men's Black Tennis Oxford, corrugated rubber soles with leather insoles. Sizes, 6 to 11. Per pair, 85c.

No. 31471. Boys' Black Tennis Oxford, corrugated rubber soles, with leather insoles. Sizes, 1 to 5; weight, 15 oz. Per pair, 70c.

No. 31472. Ladies' Black Tennis Oxford, corrugated rubber soles, with leather insoles. Sizes, 2½ to 6; weight, 15 oz. Per pair, 70c.

CHECK TENNIS BALS.

No. 31473. Men's Check Tennis Bals, corrugated rubber soles with leather insoles. Sizes, 6 to 11; weight, 20 oz. Per pair, 95c.

No. 31474. Boys' Check Tennis Bals, corrugated rubber soles with leather insoles. Sizes, 1 to 5½; weight, 17 oz. Per pair, 90c.

No. 31475. Ladies' Check Tennis Bals, corrugated rubber soles with leather insoles. Sizes, 2½ to 6; weight, 15 oz. Per pair, 85c.

CHECK TENNIS OXFORDS.

No. 31478. Men's Check Canvas Tennis Shoes, with corrugated rubber soles, best quality. Sizes, 6 to 11; weight, 17 oz. Per pair, 85c.

No. 31479. Boys' Check Canvas Tennis Shoes, with corrugated rubber soles, best quality. Sizes, 1 to 5½; weight, 15 oz. Per pair, 70c.

No. 31480. Ladies' Check Canvas Tennis Shoes, with corrugated rubber soles, best quality. Sizes, 2½ to 6; weight, 15 oz. Per pair, 70c.

MEN'S GYMNASIUM SHOES.

No. 31481. Men's low cut canvas pumps, canvas sole, and a very popular shoe at the price. Sizes, 6 to 11. Per pair, 46c.

No. 31482. Low cut canvas slipper. Made from good canvas, leather sole, machine turned. Sizes, 6 to 11. Per pair, 94c.

WHITE CANVAS GYMNASIUM SHOE.

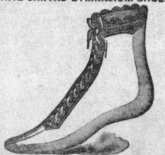

No. 31483. This shoe is made from good quality of white canvas, lace, high cut, and has a fine chamois sole which is very soft and durable. Sizes, 6 to 11. Per pair, $1.10.

We are headquarters for everything a sportsman would want.

FINE KANGAROO GYMNASIUM SHOE.

No. 31490. This shoe is made for those who wish something extremely fine, from the finest kangaroo skin, lace, genuine hand made, and has the elkskin sole, which is very light and durable. Is also used for boxing. Sizes, 6 to 11. Per pair, $3.15.

PROFESSIONAL RUNNING SHOES.

No. 31491. Made from the finest selected calf-skin, lace nearly to the toe, genuine hand sewed, six spikes, very light and extremely well made. In fact they are made for professional use. Sizes, 6 to 10. Price, per pair, $4.15.

MEDIUM RUNNING SHOES.

No. 31493. Made same style as No. 3369, from fine selected calf, very light, glove fitting, machine sewed, five spikes. Sizes, 6 to 10. Price, per pair, $2.65.

JUMPING SHOE.

No. 31494. This shoe is made expressly for jumping and hurdling, from the very finest kangaroo, hand sewed, glove fitting, and we guarantee it to be equal to any ever sold. Sizes, 6 to 10. Price, per pair, $5.50.

FOOTBALL SHOES.

No. 31495. Made from fine quality of tan grain leather, machine sewed, thigh cut lace, best quality sole, leather cleats on heel and sole, well padded at the ankles, and if you play football you certainly should not be without them. Sizes, 6 to 10. Price, per pair, $4.10.

MEN'S CRICKETING SHOES.

No. 31500. Made from the finest white duck, high cut lace, brass spikes, firmly riveted in heel and sole, a shoe which is very comfortable and durable. Sizes, 6 to 10. Per pair, $4.60.

XXX PROFESSIONAL CLOG SHOES.

No. 31501. The XXX Professional Clog Shoe is made from the finest quality of leather, by hand, has one piece wood sole, comes in black, and is guaranteed to be equal to any shoe on the market. Sizes, 6 to 10; full width. Per pair, $2.40. Jingles for above, per set, 25c.

MEN'S BICYCLE SHOES.

No. 31507. Men's Bicycle Shoes, made from good quality black leather, machine sewed, medium toe, all solid, and a good durable shoe for the price. Sizes, 6 to 11. Price, per pair, $1.68.

MEN'S FINE BICYCLE BALS.

No. 31508. Made from an extra fine selection of dull dongola kid, hand sewed, medium toe, no lining, laced nearly to the toe, corrugated soles of the very best leather, and a shoe which can be worn on the street, and always looks neat. Sizes, 6 to 11; widths, C, D, E and EE. Price, per pair, $2.25.

MEN'S TAN BICYCLE SHOES.

No. 31509. Made same style as the one above, from the best grade of tan or russet leather, hand sewed, all solid, corrugated soles of the very best grade, and is the most handsome bicycle shoe we quote. Sizes, 6 to 11; widths, C, D, E and EE. Price, per pair, $2.45.

BICYCLE OXFORDS.

The Electric.

No. 31511. This featherweight Bicycle Oxford is made from light kangaroo calf, extra light weight sole, very flexible, just the shoe for fast riding, can also be used for all kinds of athletic exercises. Sizes, 6 to 10. Price, per pair, $1.35.

No. 31512. Made from fine grade of dull dongola kid, lace nearly to the toe, machine sewed, corrugated sole, and for those who wish a low shoe, is certainly a beauty. Sizes, 6 to 11. Price, per pair, $1.75.

LADIES' BICYCLE SHOE.

No. 31513. Made from good quality dull dongola, sewed corrugated sole, made of the best sole leather, lace, high cut, and a shoe which is comfortable and can be worn on the street. Sizes, 2½ to 7; widths, D, E, and EE. Price, per pair, $1.60.

LADIES' AND GENTS' BICYCLE LEGGINS.

We take pleasure in presenting this season the most complete line of bicycle leggins carried by any house in existence. We have placed very large orders early and in fact have most of our goods in stock at the present time.

We quote prices on single pairs and also by the dozen so that any bicycle club wishing to buy in full dozen lots can buy at less than the regular wholesale price. When ordering leggins be sure to state the size of shoe worn.

No. 31515. Ladies' bicycle leggins made from very fine canvas, come just below the knee, and the canvas being very fine twill looks almost like a fine clay worsted. Colors, brown, drab and black; sizes, 1 to 7. Per pair, 40c; per dozen pairs, $4.50.

lightweight, canvas uppers. They sold for six dollars a pair, and only rich people could buy them.

A travel writer named James Greenwood noticed how quietly people walked when they wore these rubber and canvas shoes. He called the shoes "sneakers" because it was so easy to sneak around in them. Other people called them "felonies" because they were so quiet that it was easy to commit crimes while wearing them!

Shoemakers began to design sneakers for running and for playing tennis as well as for croquet. They also invented new machines that made sneakers more quickly and cheaply. By 1896 sneakers sold for less than one dollar a pair, and many more Americans could afford to buy them.

Soon several companies were making and selling sneakers. These companies included Spalding, Converse, Goodrich, U.S. Rubber, and Hood River. Sneakers were mainly popular with people who played sports. But that changed after 1916 when the U.S. Rubber Company introduced Keds.

The first Keds were nothing new or fancy. They were made with thin, black rubber soles and chestnut brown canvas that came up over the ankles. The design was simple and the colors plain, but the

By the late 1800s the shoe industry had discovered ways to make sneakers more cheaply. This page from the 1896 Sears catalog advertised boys' rubber-soled tennis sneakers, which sold for 70 cents a pair.

sneakers sold very well. For the first time, sneakers were marketed toward children and priced so that many families could buy them. This marketing plan worked, and Keds were a huge success.

The first basketball shoes—made by Converse in 1917—also became a success story. The Converse All Stars were canvas, high-topped sneakers. Their rubber soles helped prevent players from slipping on the courts. Most of these early Converse sneakers sold to teenagers and adults, who wore them mainly when playing basketball.

Four years later, Converse designed a new high-topped basketball sneaker. It was named the Chuck Taylor All Star model. Chuck Taylor was a popular basketball star who played in the 1920s and 1930s, and Converse was the only brand of sneakers he would wear.

At this time, some basketball players wanted lowcut sneakers so their ankles could move easier than with the high-topped shoes. Converse sales agent Grady Lewis had an answer. He simply cut down a high-topped sneaker and had his wife sew a seam along the trimmed top. The lowcut basketball shoe was born!

By the middle of the 1930s, the best-selling brands

of sneakers were Converse, Pro Keds, Red Ball, and PF Flyers. Many of these (and other sneaker companies, too) were owned by tire companies such as Uniroyal, Dunlop, and Goodrich.

Shoe companies worked hard to make their sneakers better. They made them with non-slip soles, suction-cup soles, ripple soles, arch supports, and heel supports to make it easier to play sports. They also made sneakers in different colors for people who cared about how their shoes looked.

In the early 1940s, during World War II, the shoe industry changed in

Chuck Taylor—a basketball star in the 1920s and 1930s— wearing Converse All Stars.

another way. *Synthetic*, or human-made, rubber replaced natural rubber.

Rubber is very important during wartime. It's needed to make tires for jeeps and trucks. Before World War II, most natural rubber came from the Far

In 1937, most of these New York City children had chosen to wear sneakers to play in.

East, but during the war, the Japanese captured the lands where it was produced.

Having a supply of rubber helped the Japanese. They used it to make tires for their vehicles. They also made rubber-soled sneakers for their soldiers, who wore them on the battlefield.

The United States was forced to come up with a way of making its own rubber without using the natural product. Soon a team of scientists began to work on this important wartime project. They found ways to make rubber using a mixture of *butadiene* (a gas), coal tar, and petroleum. By the end of the war, the United States was making more than 2 billion pounds of synthetic rubber a year!

After the war, the lifestyle of many Americans changed a great deal. The standard of living improved, so people had more free time and more money to spend. Some of their free time was spent watching a fascinating new invention—the television. Among the television shows were sports programs, which increased people's interest in playing sports. Because of all these changes in America, more people than ever before bought sneakers.

Canvas basketball sneakers led the way in sales. At first, high tops sold the most, but soon lowcuts were just as popular. Both styles were comfortable, inexpensive, and long-lasting.

By the 1950s, sneakers were no longer being used mainly for sports. Men, women, and especially children now wore sneakers for casual, everyday footwear. Sneakers were comfortable, and they looked good, too. For the first time, people began to wear sneakers for fashion.

In less than one century, the sneaker business had grown from a few small companies to a multi-million dollar industry. But this was just the beginning.

Footnotes

■ Shoes have been a sign of fashion for centuries. In the 1300s, men in Europe wore shoes called crackowes. The toes of these shoes were so long that they had to be fastened to the knees to keep the men from tripping over them.

■ In 1868, sneakers cost six dollars a pair. At that time, six dollars could buy a saddle, a plow, or a coal stove.

■ The Chuck Taylor All Star model is the most popular sneaker in history.

■ Keds was the first company to design a colorful sneaker. In the 1920s it introduced a blue sneaker.

3

New, Improved Sneakers

When you went to buy a pair of sneakers in the 1950s, you didn't have many choices. At that time, you could pick from a couple of different brands and colors. You could choose between high tops and lowcuts, too. But there were very few styles, and most of the sneakers had thin, rubber soles and canvas uppers. And that's the way sneakers stayed until training shoes became popular.

Training shoes were first made after World War II ended in 1945. They were developed mainly by two German companies, Adidas and Puma, for athletes to wear while stretching and exercising before playing a sport. The first training shoes had rubber soles and leather uppers.

Leather wasn't new to sports shoes. The material was stiff and heavy, but also sturdy and long-lasting.

There weren't many styles of sneakers to choose from in the 1950s, but two boys in this class chose high tops.

Over the years it had been used in baseball, football, track, and boxing shoes, both in the uppers and in the soles. Early leather sport shoes were not true "sneakers," since it was impossible to sneak around in the heavy, noisy shoes. But the new, rubber-soled training shoes were quieter. People could now call these shoes sneakers too.

By the 1960s, training shoes began to be made with canvas uppers. Athletes loved these lightweight training shoes. Soon, the shoes grew popular with the general public as well and became fashionable.

In 1962, a Boston shoe company called New Balance created the modern running shoe. The New Balance Trackster had ripple soles to help prevent slipping, leather uppers for added support, and a rubber heel *wedge* to help absorb shock. Together, these features made the Trackster very popular with runners.

Meanwhile, on the west coast, Bill Bowerman was hard at work. Bowerman was the track coach at the University of Oregon. He was so dissatisfied with the track shoes available in the 1950s and 1960s that he designed and made shoes for the athletes on his team.

Bowerman knew that his handmade sneakers were better than the ones on the market. They were lighter and they fit better. The real proof was that his athletes broke records while wearing them.

In 1967, a Japanese shoe manufacturing company called Tiger produced Bowerman's Marathon model. The Marathon was the first sneaker in history with a

The New Balance Trackster.

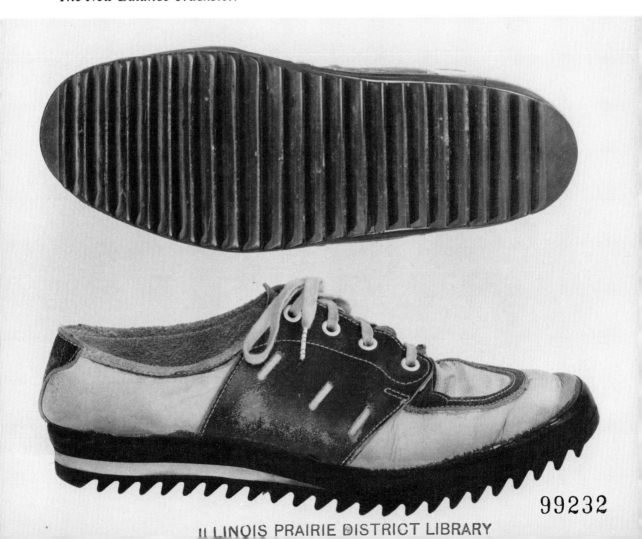

99232

nylon upper. This synthetic material was tough, lightweight, and allowed sweat to dry quickly.

The next year, a runner named Jeff Johnson worked with Bowerman to design a padded *midsole* cushion. This cushion extended the full length of the

Bill Bowerman (on the right) *with one of his track team athletes in the 1960s.*

sneaker. It helped absorb shock and made the shoe more comfortable, especially when running.

Meanwhile, the Adidas company in Germany was trying to improve basketball sneakers. In 1968 it produced a basketball shoe with a rubber shell sole. This sole had a deep cradle in which the foot rested. It did a better job of supporting and holding the foot in place, and it felt more comfortable, too. Basketball players around the world welcomed the improvement. In fact, half of the players in the 1968 NCAA championship basketball game between Houston and UCLA wore the new Adidas sneakers.

Adidas didn't stop at improving basketball shoes. It worked hard to improve all of its footwear. At the 1968 Olympics, more than 80 percent of the athletes wore Adidas shoes.

1968 was also the year Dr. Kenneth Cooper's book, *Aerobics*, was published. The book gave advice for becoming and staying physically fit, and it helped increase Americans' interest in fitness.

The 1972 Olympics added to this interest. For the first time, an American runner won the 26.2 mile (42.2 kilometer) marathon. Frank Shorter won the race, and he became a symbol for America's new fitness craze.

As more people exercised, the need for better

sneakers grew. Bill Bowerman, who had helped to start the Nike shoe company, set out to improve sneakers even more. He wanted to create a new sole that was lightweight and that would help keep runners from slipping.

After trying many different things, Bowerman poured some rubber into his family's waffle iron. The smell was terrible, and it almost started a fire. Yet the sole was just what Bowerman wanted, except for one thing—he couldn't get it out of the waffle iron!

That was only a minor problem, however. Nike soon perfected the design of Bowerman's "waffle" soles. These lightweight, non-slip soles were the first of many improved soles that helped runners.

Just how popular was running during the 1970s? Consider the Boston marathon, one of the most well known races in the world. In 1970, 1,000 runners entered the race. By 1979, the number of runners increased to more than 9,000! In addition to these marathon runners, more than 17 million Americans were running regularly.

This new interest in running changed the sneaker industry, bringing many more companies into the competition for sales. These companies included Avia, Brooks, Etonic, Osaga, Reebok, and Saucony.

In the 1970s, millions of Americans began to run regularly to keep fit.

The increase in the number of runners helped bring about changes in sneakers. In 1974, the Monarch Rubber Company invented a new material called *EVA*— ethylene vinyl acetate. EVA is a foam made from plastic, filled with gas bubbles, which is lighter and a better shock absorber than rubber. Brooks was the first company to use EVA in its sneakers. Today, most sneaker midsoles are made of EVA.

In the mid-1970s, sneaker companies began to hire scientists to help improve their products. Using high-speed photography, scientists were able to study exactly how the foot moves. This information led to more sneaker improvements. In 1975, New Balance made a sneaker with a flared heel—a sole that's wider at the ground than where it meets the upper. This flared heel helped keep the foot stable when running.

Many other changes in sneakers occurred during the 1970s. For instance, *insoles* (cushioned pads inside the sneaker, on which the feet rest) were made softer, and *heel counters* (plastic cups) were added to help support the heels. Runners around the world appreciated these improvements.

If the 1970s was known for running, the 1980s must be remembered for *aerobics.* In the early 1980s, millions of people, mostly women, took aerobic dance classes as a way to stay fit. A British shoe company, Reebok, designed a soft, comfortable leather sneaker for aerobic dancers. Besides being comfortable, these sneakers were designed so they looked fashionable. Now, the way sneakers looked became as important as how they helped people exercise and perform in sports.

The fashion trend in sneakers continued and grew with L.A. Gear, an American sneaker company. Starting in 1982, L.A. Gear designed sneakers with buckles, sequins, and rhinestones. Were these sneakers popular? Yes! L.A. Gear's sales rose from 9 million dollars in 1984 to 600 million dollars in 1989!

At the end of the 1980s, shoe companies improved sneakers even more. Reebok made a sneaker that could be pumped with air for extra support and

The Pump, created by Reebok in the 1980s, could be pumped with air.

comfort. Asics Tiger created a sneaker with gel in its sole for added cushioning. Nike created the cross-trainer, a shoe that could be used for several different sports. Avia designed a sneaker with a plastic spring in its heel, to help absorb shock.

In 1990, there were more than 500 models and 1,000 styles of sneakers. Choosing a pair was no longer the simple decision that it had been in 1890!

Footnotes

In 1967, the New Balance Trackster became the first athletic shoe made in different width sizes.

Nike was the winged goddess of victory in Greek mythology.

The Nike swoosh trademark was designed by Carolyn Davidson, a Portland State University art student, for a fee of $35.

By 1980, nearly half of the world's sneakers were being made in Korea and Taiwan because of low labor costs in those countries.

In 1981, the New Balance 990 became the first sneaker to cost more than $100.

The average price for a pair of sneakers in 1989 was about $27.

4 Sneakers Today

Do you want to buy some sneakers? You're in luck. Today, there are sneakers for sale everywhere, and there's a style for everyone.

If you don't want to spend much money, you can get a pair of sneakers for less than $10.

If you want to spend more, that's no problem either. There are sneakers that sell for more than $150 a pair.

Today's sneakers come in many colors, models, and styles. There is a sneaker made for almost every known activity, too.

The most popular are basketball shoes. Think of what your feet do when you play basketball. They run, jump, start, stop, and turn quickly. Basketball sneakers are designed to make it easier for your feet to do these things. The leather uppers on high tops give your

There are sneaker styles available today to suit everyone's taste.

ankles the support they need for running and jumping. Heel counters help keep your feet from twisting, and the hard rubber soles help grip the court. They also aid the player in making fast, smooth turns.

Basketball shoes have extra cushioning, too. This helps absorb the jolt of jumping. This jolt can be from three to five times the player's body weight. For professional basketball players who jump very high, the pressure can be as much as 10 times their body weight.

Cross-training shoes are the second-most popular sneakers. They are designed to be worn

Professional basketball players must wear basketball shoes, which help absorb the jolt of jumping.

for more than one activity, such as basketball, racquetball, and aerobics. Cross-training shoes have cushioned soles necessary for running and jumping, and hard rubber along their sides to support the feet when moving from side-to-side. Some cross-training sneakers have adjustable straps for added support.

The third-most popular sneakers are tennis shoes. Tennis players run forward, backward, and side-to-side, making many quick starts and stops. Tennis sneakers have hard soles that help the shoes last through the skidding and scraping of many tennis matches. They also have extra layers of leather over the toes, because some players drag the front of their sneakers against the court when serving the ball.

Running shoes are the fourth-most popular sneakers. They are made to protect your body from the pounding it takes when jogging or running. Thick cushions on the soles keep the runner from being injured or feeling sore after his or her run. The tread on the *outsole* also absorbs shock and helps prevent the runner from slipping on different surfaces.

Basketball, cross-training, tennis, and running shoes are only four of the many types of sneakers you can buy today. You can buy aerobic, bicycling, and cheerleading sneakers, too. There are also sneakers made for fencing, gymnastics, table tennis, volleyball, rock-climbing, walking, wrestling, boardsailing, and many more activities.

Does this mean you have to do the activity the sneaker was made for if you're going to buy it? No. In fact, most people don't. At least 80 percent of the sneakers sold in the United States are not used for the activity for which they were made.

Why do so many people have sneakers if they aren't going to use them for what they were made? To answer that question, start by looking at your foot.

Your foot is an amazing creation. It acts like a platform to help you stand up. It also helps you move the 70,000 miles that you will walk and run during your lifetime. That's as far as walking nearly three times around the world!

Your foot is made up of bones, *tendons*, and *ligaments*. Tendons are tough cords of tissue that connect bones to muscles. Ligaments are strong, flexible bands of tissue that connect bones to each other. Bones, tendons, and ligaments work together to help your foot move, and to protect it.

In every step that you take, your tendons stretch, your bones spread out, and your foot flattens. When you lift your foot, the tendons snap back, and your bones move closer together. This action puts the "spring" in your walk, and helps protect your body from the forces of walking, running, and jumping.

Footwear was invented to help protect this amazing creation, your foot. Some shoes, such as the earliest sandals, gave little protection but were flexible and easy to wear. Other footwear, such as the armor worn by knights in the Middle Ages, gave much protection but was very stiff and made movement difficult.

Today's sneakers offer your feet a comfortable balance. They protect your feet and yet allow easy movement. That's why so many people buy them.

People also buy sneakers because shoe companies work hard to sell their products. They spend more than $200 million each year promoting and advertising them. They sponsor races, host sports clinics, and give their shoes to college basketball teams. Most of the $200 million, though, is spent on advertising.

Many shoe companies pay professional athletes to wear their sneakers. That's great advertising because millions of people watch professional sports. Some companies hire superstars to appear on their television ads, too. But these superstars don't have to be athletes. Rock stars also advertise sneakers.

Does advertising work? Do people buy more sneakers because of all the ads? The shoe companies seem to think so, and there's evidence to prove that it does work.

Between 1985 and 1989, as these companies spent more on advertising, sales grew by about 23 percent a year. In 1989, more than 150 million pairs of sneakers were sold in the United States. That's twice as many sneakers as were sold only five years earlier!

Advertising has helped shoe companies sell nearly $10 billion worth of sneakers a year, but this might not be good for everyone who buys them. Advertising makes people want sneakers more. At times, this desire leads to crimes.

Crimes involving sneakers have been reported since 1985 in cities around the United States. Americans have robbed money to buy sneakers, and they have stolen them from stores. They have hurt—even killed other people—for a pair of sneakers.

Some people blame the shoe companies for these crimes. They say sneaker prices are too high, and that advertisements are aimed at Americans who can't afford to buy this footwear. Shoe companies don't agree. There are less expensive sneakers to buy, they argue. People, they say, can choose to buy what they

Some shoe companies hire superstars—including rock stars such as Michael Jackson—to advertise their sneakers.

want and should spend what they are able to afford.

Who is really to blame for these crimes? There is no clear answer. What's clear, though, is that the crimes show how highly valued sneakers have become today.

Footnotes

Each of your feet has 26 bones. Your feet have about one-fourth of all the bones in your body.

The tendons in your feet are like rubber bands. In the first century A.D., the Romans used animal tendons to power their rock-throwing catapults.

Your feet grow about one-third of an inch each year, when you are between the ages of 4 and 11. That equals one shoe size every year.

If you are right-handed, your left foot is probably longer than your right foot. This happens because you use your left foot more for support, which causes its ligaments and muscles to grow longer.

In 1989, Nike paid basketball star Michael Jordan more than $1.5 million to help sell the company's sneakers.

Discount stores sell the most sneakers today.

Nearly half of all shoes sold today are sneakers.

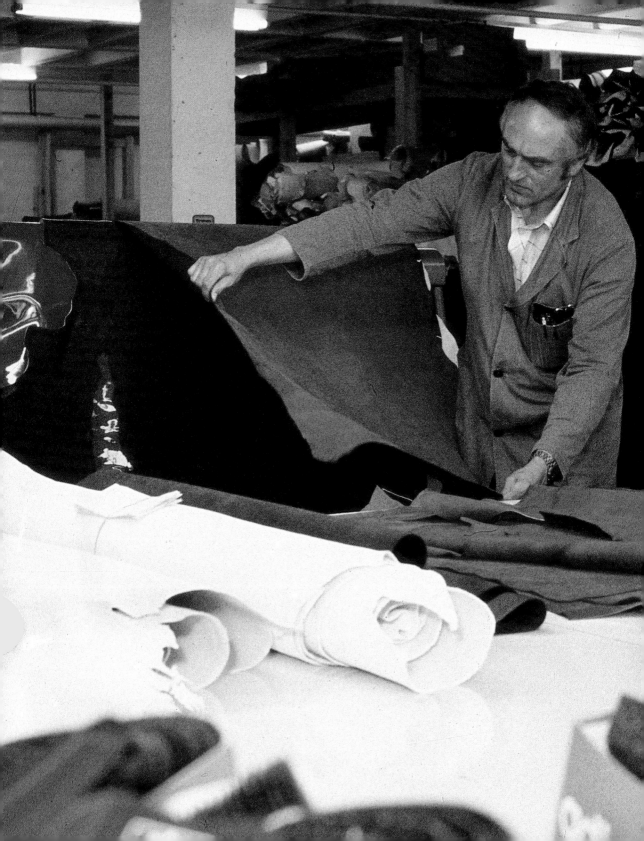

5 Making Sneakers

Sneakers may look simple, but they're not so simple to make. It takes special machines and many skilled people to create a pair of sneakers.

At the sneaker factory, all of the shoe parts arrive in the receiving room. They come from different factories around the world. Canvas, nylon, and leather arrive in large pieces or on rolls. Big sheets of foam appear too, as well as sheets of hard rubber stamped with tread designs. The foam will become wedges and midsoles, and the hard rubber will be used for outsoles.

Not all sneaker parts come to the receiving room on rolls or as large sheets. Some arrive in small pieces. These pieces, called *findings*, are very important in sneaker-making too. Heel counters, laces, and arch pads (which are called *cookies*) are just some of the findings needed to make a pair of sneakers.

In the receiving room, a factory worker inspects rolls of fabric.

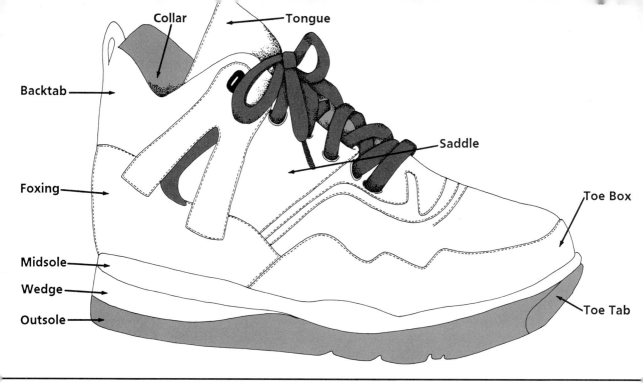

Collar

Tongue

Backtab

Saddle

Foxing

Toe Box

Midsole

Wedge

Outsole

Toe Tab

This drawing shows several of the many parts of a modern sneaker.

After the parts enter the receiving room, they are inspected and stored. They are now ready to be used in making sneakers.

First, the ten main pieces of the upper are cut out of leather, nylon, or canvas. Metal devices called *dies* stamp out the pieces. Dies come in many different shapes and have sharp, metal edges. But even with these sharp edges, the nylon, canvas, and leather are tough to cut, and powerful presses must help. These presses push down the dies with thousands of pounds of pressure to slice through the material.

Besides cutting out the pieces, the presses also make little nicks on the material. These nicks are useful in the next step of sneaker-making.

When all of the upper pieces have been cut, they are sent to the fitting room. This room is filled with the hum of sewing machines where workers sew the pieces together. They use the nicks in the material to line up the pieces and sew them straight. One worker sews on a piece, then passes it to another worker who sews on another piece. One upper might be sewn by more than 20 different workers!

After the uppers are sewn, a machine punches lace holes in them. Now, the sneakers are ready for *lasting*, which gives the sneakers their shape.

Inside the lasting room, there isn't a sewing machine in sight.

All of the upper pieces are sewn together in the fitting room.

Instead, there are heavy lasting machines and a strong smell of *cement*, or glue, in the air. To begin, a heel counter is slipped between the layers of heel material. Then the whole upper is heated. Heating makes it easier to stretch the material. Meanwhile, a thin board made of wood fibers, called the *insole board*, is tacked to the bottom of a *last*—a plastic mold shaped like a foot. The worker fits the warm upper around the last and sends it to a lasting machine.

The lasting machine pulls the upper tightly around the last. The machine spreads cement between the upper and the insole board. Then it uses its metal "fingers" to hold the two parts together until the cement dries. The upper is now ready to be joined to the sole.

In another part of the factory, machines stamp outsoles out of rubber, and midsoles and wedges out of foam. The pieces are then cemented together to become sneaker soles.

There are many ways to join the sole to the upper. It can be tacked, stapled, or sewn, but the most common method is gluing.

A worker spreads cement over the top of the midsole. Then the sole and the upper are placed together and put into a high pressure press. The press squeezes the two parts together for a short time until the glue dries.

The shoe now looks like a sneaker, but it's not quite finished. The last must be removed. Luckily, it has a hinge in it. The hinge allows the last to be bent

The upper is now joined to the sole.

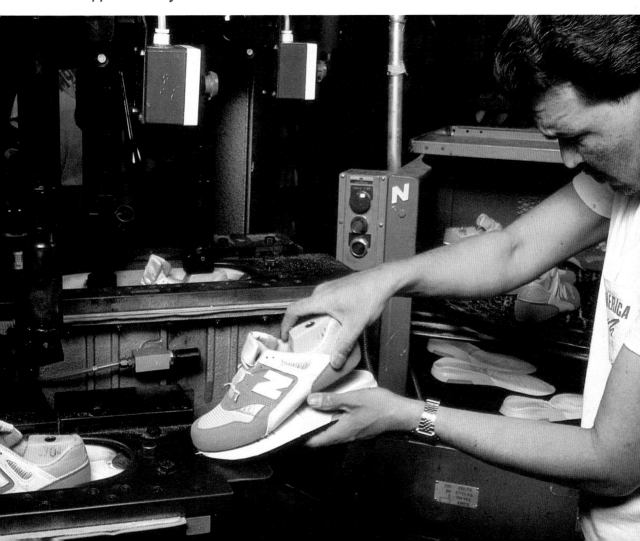

in two pieces and easily taken out of the sneaker.

When the last has been removed, the insole, cookie, and laces are added. Then the sneaker is inspected to make sure that all the parts fit and that all the extra cement has been cleaned off.

Sneakers that pass careful inspection are matched up in pairs and put into boxes. The boxes are then shipped to stores around the world. It's in one of these stores that a special pair of sneakers will find its way to your feet.

Footnotes

■ Some sneaker factories make as many as 300,000 pairs of sneakers a day.

■ It costs $15 to $20 to manufacture a pair of sneakers that sells for $60 to $100.

■ Sneakers are always boxed with the right shoe on top of the left shoe. Manufacturers believe the right sneaker looks better.

■ The strongest leather used in sneakers is made from kangaroo skin. It can stand as much as 4,000 pounds of pressure per square inch before tearing.

Kangaroos are *endangered*, which means that their remaining numbers are threatened. For this reason, it is against the law to bring kangaroo skin into the United States.

■ Adi Dassler, founder of Adidas, was one of the most famous shoe and sneaker designers. When he died in 1978, he had more than 800 patents to his name.

■ Nearly all—97 per-cent—of the sneakers sold in the United States are made in other countries.

6 Sneakers of the Future

At this very moment, shoes of the future are being created. And just as today's sneakers are different from those of the past, sneakers of the future will be different from the ones you're wearing now.

Some changes in tomorrow's sneakers will make a difference in the way they work for you. These changes might give your foot more protection or allow your foot more flexibility. Most changes, though, will be in fashion.

Tomorrow's sneakers begin as ideas. Some come from sales clerks in stores who know what people want, such as a new style or color. Other ideas come from *biomechanists*, scientists who study the human body in motion. Some of these scientists film people's feet in motion, using high-speed photography. They play back the film in slow motion, watching the

When this child is ten years old, the sneakers she'll buy will likely be quite different from the model she's wearing today.

smallest parts of each movement. Biomechanists know the special needs of the human foot. They use this information to help create new sneakers.

Sneaker designers have their own ideas for new shoes, too. They take suggestions from professional athletes, then combine these with their own imaginations to create new designs. Designers do more than think up ideas. They make detailed drawings of their sneakers and then build models of them. These handmade, full-sized models are called *prototypes*. Each sneaker prototype is carefully considered by a team of people. The designer, a person from the shoe company's marketing department, and a person from the company's development department make up the team. If they are satisfied with the prototype, about 100 pairs of the sneakers are made. These samples will be tested. Sneaker companies don't want to manufacture millions of pairs of sneakers without testing a smaller number first.

Some of the sneakers are tested by people. Companies select people who would most likely buy the type of sneaker being tested. They wear the samples and then answer questions about them. This is called "wear testing."

Other tests are performed by machines in labo-

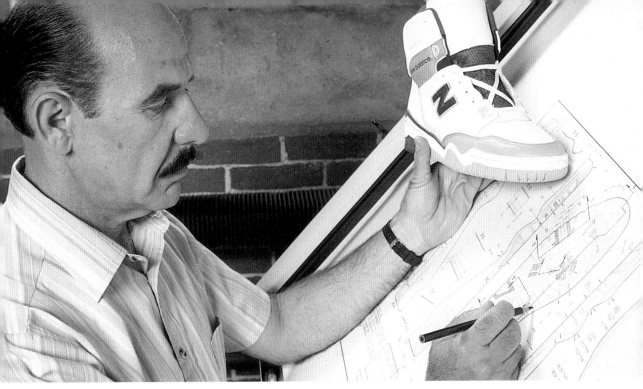

Designers make detailed drawings of new sneaker styles, then build prototypes from the drawings.

ratories. One machine tests how flexible the sneaker is, and another measures how much shock the shoe can absorb. These are just two of many laboratory tests performed.

When all of the tests are finished, the results are studied by the team. These three people make the final decision about the new design—whether or not it will be manufactured and sold.

What kinds of sneakers will be created and sold in the future? There will be many more designs than there are today. They will be made with stronger and lighter materials, and replaceable parts such as outsoles. Tomorrow's sneakers will heat or cool your feet, or even change colors, depending on the outside air temperature!

Some designers believe that sneakers of the future will have computers in them. Just imagine what this could mean. You put on your sneakers, and they automatically adjust the tightness of the laces, the insole support, and the cushioning according to your size and weight. By pushing a button, air fills small bags around your ankles, straps tighten around the sides of your feet, and the heels adjust. You are now ready to play basketball.

The future is sure to bring many changes to sneakers. But there is one fact that won't change—sneakers will always be the shoes that millions of people choose.

Footnotes

Regular video cameras take between 30 and 60 pictures a second. Biomechanists use cameras that take as many as 200 pictures a second.

Sneaker designers are designing shoes today that people will wear one to two years from now.

Nike designer Tinker Hatfield created the sneakers that appeared in the movie *Back to the Future, Part II*.

Changes are made to most models of sneakers every six months.

A Sneakers Time Line

1600 B.C. Babylonians make the first moccasins

A.D. 1400 Indian peoples of Central and South America use cahuchu sap to make waterproof shoes

1770 Joseph Priestly, an English chemist, discovers that cahuchu sap rubs off pencil marks; this sap is named "rubber"

1839 Charles Goodyear discovers vulcanization

1868 Croquet shoes are made with rubber soles and canvas uppers; they sell for six dollars a pair

1873 The term "sneaker" is first used

1897 Sneakers are made mainly by machines; their price drops to 60 cents a pair

1917 The first basketball sneakers—Converse All Stars—are made by Converse

1940s Synthetic rubber is made in the United States

1950s Sneakers become fashionable

1960s Training shoes become popular

1962 New Balance makes the Trackster, the first modern running shoe

1967 Tiger makes the Marathon model, the first sneaker with a nylon upper

1970s Millions of Americans run for fitness

1982 Reebok makes the first aerobic sneaker

1987 Nike creates the first cross-training sneaker

1989 L.A. Gear makes 600 million dollars selling fashionable sneakers

1990 Matt Greenhalgh, of Greenwich, Rhode Island, wins the Odor-Eaters International Rotten Sneaker Contest

For More Information

For more information about the Odor-Eaters International Rotten Sneaker Contest, write to:
Odor-Eaters Rotten Sneaker Contest
1101 Westchester Avenue
White Plains, NY 10604
(enclose 50 cents for postage and handling)

For more information about sneakers and particular brands, write to:
Marketing Department
Adidas USA
15 Independence Boulevard
Warren, NJ 07060

Consumer Relations Department
Avia
P.O. Box 23309
Portland, OR 97223
1-800-345-AVIA

Advertising Department
Converse, Inc.
1 Fordham Road
North Reading, MA 01864
Consumer Affairs Department

L.A. Gear
4221 Redwood Avenue
Los Angeles, CA 90066-5619

Corporate Communications
New Balance
38 Everett Street
Boston, MA 02134

Consumer Services
Nike
1 Bowerman Drive
Beaverton, OR 97005
1-800-344-NIKE

Consumer Relations Department
Reebok International Limited
100 Technology Center Drive
Stoughton, MA 02072

Department of Communications
Sporting Goods Manufacturers'
Association
200 Castlewood Drive
North Palm Beach, FL 33408

Places to visit:
Adidas Sport Shoe Museum
Adi Dassler St. 2
Herzogenaurach,Germany

Rotten Sneaker Hall of Fumes
Montpelier Department of Recreation
Montpelier, VT 05602

Glossary

aerobics (ar-OH-biks)—exercises that strengthen the lungs and heart, by increasing the intake of oxygen

biomechanist (by-oh-MEK-in-ist)—a scientist who studies the human body in motion

butadiene (byut-uh-DIE-een)—a gas used in making synthetic rubber

canvas—a heavy cloth woven from cotton

cement—glue; used in joining sneaker parts

cookie—a padded arch support inside a sneaker

curing (KYUR-ing)—mixing sulphur with rubber and heating the mixture; this process (also called vulcanizing) makes rubber more useful in all weather conditions

die—a metal device used in stamping sneaker parts out of nylon, canvas, or leather

endangered—animals or plants that are so few in number that they could become extinct

findings—small sneaker parts

EVA—ethylene vinyl acetate, a foam filled with gas bubbles; most sneaker midsoles are made of EVA

heel counter—a plastic cup in the heel of a sneaker; heel counters help control the back of the foot

insole—a cushioned pad on which the foot rests inside a sneaker

insole board—a thin board made of wood fibers; the upper is glued to the insole board during the lasting process

last—a plastic form shaped like a foot

lasting—the process of pulling the upper tightly around a last, which gives the sneaker its shape

ligament (LIG-uh-ment)—a strong, flexible band of tissue that connects bones or holds organs in place

midsole—a padded layer in a sneaker sole

outsole—the bottom layer of a sneaker sole; the layer that touches the ground

prototype (PROHT-uh-tipe)—a full-size, original model; this model serves as a pattern for making other objects that are just like it

sole—the bottom part of a sneaker, made up of an outsole, a wedge, and a midsole

sulphur (SUL-fuhr)—a yellow mineral; used in curing rubber

synthetic (sin-THET-ik)—made artificially with chemicals

tendon (TEN-duhn)—a tough cord of tissue that connects bone with muscle

upper—the top part of a sneaker

vulcanizing (VOL-kin-i-zing)—*see* curing

wedge—a cushioned layer in the sole of a sneaker; the wedge is between the midsole and the outsole

Index